Seeds of Leadership,
Cultivating the Culture into a Fruitful Harvest

By

Joaquin Urrutia

Seeds of Leadership

DEDICATION

To the leaders that inspired the seeds in this short
read.

Jerry Blake was an inspiration to hone my skills as a
machinist and the mindset to never stop learning.

Dave Hamilton was truly a leader, inherently having the
ability to motivate others to excel.

Cecil Peters, a leader of industry that recognized the
abilities in others and encouraged everyone that
surrounded him.

To my wife, she is the best part of my life.

And above all, the Lord, for all the blessings of working
with all the beautiful people that I have had the
opportunity to learn from.

Table of Contents

ACKNOWLEDGMENTS

To the managers that did not support trust, the ones that
led by intimidation, the lessons learned from you support
the content of what not to do!

Introduction

If you are in a position of authority and supervising others, you should read this book. It is time to recognize, take responsibility, adapt, and succeed in the position that has been given to you. If the culture of the department is dysfunctional and not performing at the level it should be, the seeds within this book will help elevate the level of performance. Expectations of employees performing at their best, requires leaders of departments to cultivate the path to success.

Seed: Change in culture takes time, as the soil needs to be turned, fertilized, and seeded.

I am sure you have already a few mistakes in your career than you can remember. Moving forward you can learn from all those mistakes if you cared enough to keep a log of them. Maybe you went to school as I did and have a degree in management and think you know it all, you are highly mistaken!

Seed: Having a mindset and desire to improve, requires humility and respect of others abilities.

Seed: Life is full of lessons, are you learning from the past and applying the wisdom to the future?

Seed: Recognition of our weakness is an opportunity to improve our abilities to lead others.

Or maybe you are part of the selected few that has a mentor that has prepared you to be in a leadership role. I am talking about someone that has taken the time to coach, guide, equip, and train you to be successful leading others. Someone that has taken you under his or her wing and could see your potential. These are the unicorns of the workforce, they are out there but hard to find!

I have experienced supervisors with inherit abilities of leadership and others that led by authority, teams that were dysfunctional and others that were highly productive. The lessons I have learned and the experience I have gained from working for different employers have shaped me into who I am today, someone that realizes there are too many people in charge that should not be.

Illegitimate leadership has infected many organizations and our country and this has hurt our workforce to perform at the level it is capable of!

The wisdom I am sharing is found within the stories and seeds I am giving to you. Please take them, plant them into your leadership style, and bear the fruit of investing into others.

We will never know true leadership until we have had the opportunity to work for someone that is enjoyable to work with and supports you in ways that no other manager has done before. We remember the leaders that care about developing employees, leaders that give credit when you deserve it, and protect the employees from the politics of upper management.

Seed: Discarded seeds are untapped potential.

I was twelve years old and I had a paper route with 80 customers. I recognized the demand for certain skillsets while reading the classifieds. Jobs in construction, electrical, plumbing, and machining were posted almost every week. I believed if I could learn one of these trades I would always have a job.

In my thirty plus years working for different employers I have recognized a few characteristics that good leaders have in common such as: trust, respect, they inspire and coach, they encourage and support others, they have the ability to control their emotions, and they cause employees to become engaged and take ownership of their performance. And, I have recognized what managers can and will do to destroy employees loyalty and moral. Leading to an increase in overturn, absenteeism, lowered production, loss of profit, and loss of valuable employees. If this book is able to help one manager realize what they have been doing wrong, this book is a success.

Seed: Measuring ones success should be taken from what he or she has done for others.

Seed: Every conversation with any employee is an opportunity to cultivate culture, if your interaction is not watering the seed, your interaction is drying it out.

Chapter 1

Lessons from Mistakes

It was 1988; I was working for a cabinet shop in Riverside California. The shop's staff consisted of the owner and myself. I was his apprentice cabinetmaker and I enjoyed working with wood. My girlfriend would smell me and say, "the smell of wood is like a cologne of a working man." While working for Ed, he identified my ability to work safely and efficiently. Ed recognized I had a natural ability for finishing furniture, I had learned this skillset at a young age while working with my stepdad in the garage.

One day while working on a Saturday, one of my friends showed up at the shop. He asked me if I could leave early and go to the beach. I asked Ed if I could leave early and he said, "sure, just finish drilling all the bed rails on the cart." I looked at the cart and told my buddy no problem, I finished them in thirty minutes and we left.

When I arrived to work on Tuesday after school, Ed had a look of disappointment on his face and asked me to follow him. He pointed at the cart of bedposts that I drilled out and asked me if I saw anything wrong with them, I said no. He then explained that I drilled them out to fit all styles of beds, which means they had extra holes, a lot of extra holes! Ed said I am lucky that he had time to cool off because when he saw the mistake he had picked up one of the posts and through it across the shop. Ed told me that if he fired me that someone else could make the same mistake and I had a talent of finishing furniture that not all people have. To prevent the mistake from happening again I color-coded the holes on the jig.

Seeds of Leadership

Seed: Before deciding to let someone go for a mistake, think about how valuable they are and how long would it take to train someone to their level.
Seed: When an employee makes a mistake is it because they lack training, education, or experience?
Seed: Mistakes are usually lessons learned; usually they will not make the same mistake twice!

The year was 1990, I was employed as an apprentice Tool and Die Maker. I had made a mistake when I cut too much material off a piece of metal, the metal is known as O1, this is a type of tool steel. When I realized the mistake, I took it to my manager and explained the error. As he was smoking a cigarette, he took a pair of dial calipers to measure the part and looked at the blueprint. In a manner of absolute disappointment, he threw the part across the shop at the wall and in a serious tone he asked me if I liked my job and informing me that he cannot afford to pay for my mistakes. I made a mistake, which ruined the part, and we had no extra material. When this happened I realized that my manager was upset because he was under the impression I wasted his money and his time. He was financially and emotionally invested, two traits that effected his ability to control his own emotions and his ability to make sound decisions. As time passed, we became good friends and had a mutual respect for each other.

Seed: When faced with others being emotionally unstable, try to understand their motives for their behavior.
Seed: When they are really upset, wait until the storm has calmed before you try to discuss how to prevent the same mistake.
Seed: Avoid making important decisions when emotionally distracted.
Seed: To manage by fear is to suppress creativity and commitment.
Seed: Valuable lessons are usually learned from valuable mistakes.

The greatest leader that every existed was known as Jesus Christ. He was a servant leader, He put his disciples needs above His own, He is a teacher, and He speaks from experience, understanding, and application.

Seed: What made Jesus the greatest leader is what He did for others; He died for us to live eternally.

Seed: By one mans sin we are committed to death, by another mans sacrifice we are granted life.

Seed: When management equips employees with the tools and training to be successful, they are truly leading and developing employees to be their best!

While working as an instructor of a program of industrial maintenance, I recognized the lack of resources and references. I brought this to my manager's attention and her response was how did we function for all the years before I was the instructor without the additional resources and references. As time progressed I was required to write letters of validation for any purchases. I became a pro at validating the reasons of purchasing additional equipment to increase efficiency of time spent on applying the subject material. But, this also damaged my relationship with my manager, the budget was getting spent and she was not able to appear to upper management as someone that was cutting costs. I sacrificed being promoted and my future of moving up, for the benefit of my students and their training.

Seed: Servant leadership is putting your employees needs first.

Seed: Sacrificing your success for the success of others is the path of leadership.

Chapter 2

Our Words that Color Us

As I returned from lunch I heard the voices of two women yelling at each other in the hallway, one was the manager of the department and the other the administrative assistant. The conversation was driven by emotions; students and staff heard the fighting stopped by the slamming of doors. The behavior and language colored the department in a shade of ugly.

Seed: Be mindful of the words you use when arguing with others, for they will be remembered and represent your professional standing.

Seed: Words can be reactive or proactive in elevating an argument or extinguishing it.

Some organizations promote individuals into leadership positions based on their technical background and/or interviewing skills, this decision can lead to management lacking the ability to communicate effectively, the lack of social and emotional intelligence, and as a result the department becoming dysfunctional and disengaged.

Seed: When employees stop caring about their success, they stop caring about the success of the organization. The lack of caring could develop into a toxic environment.

Seed: Management's focus should be directed by what is best for the organization and not driven by the manager's emotions.

While in the eighth grade, I had an instructor that raced mini sprint cars. The class was called Power Mechanics, we learned about combustion driven motors and everyone in the class rebuilt a 5Hp Briggs and Stratton motor. Something he said about racing I never forgot. He said when your racing you have a percentage of the control, the other percentage is the other drivers, the environment, and equipment. Many managers that thought they were in control. Very much like racing and/or driving a vehicle, as a manager you have a percentage of the control. As a leader, you need to provide support that keeps the department on track to finish the race. When you are in charge, you have the ability to choose the color of the department, support your team and the color of unity!

Seed: Control is an illusion of management, while support is the reality of leadership.

Seed: Leaders are proactive and anticipate the other factors that could derail the department from achieving the goals of the organization.

Seed: Management that has a tight grip on the steering wheel will crash because of the inability to maneuver and navigate around the obstacles when achieving objectives.

The value of an employee increases as they become more experienced and/or specialized in their position. As employees become experts in their field they become proud of their accomplishments. Pride of an employee may generate a false sense of security and lead them into making decisions based on their emotions and not what is best for his or her family.

Seed: Managers and employees need to identify the benefits of humility and how it supports positive working dynamics within the team.

Seed: Collaboration of experience is a strong tool.

When a team is infected with incivility it can become destructive. Gossip, lies, insults, threats, bullying, and insecurities drive destructive forces.

Seed: Address the issues of incivility as soon as they are recognized, nobody likes pulling weeds but it is necessary to keep the soil from being overwhelmed by thorns.

Managers may become intimidated and threatened by certain employees that are highly experienced and/or educated. This leads to doubt and fear, which could influence the manager to become defensive of recommendations and make decisions that are not for the best interest of the organization. Managers that allow decisions to be made based on their feelings can cause employees to lose trust in their manager's ability to lead the department effectively.

Seed: When you are the manager do not let the position mislead your decision making capacity by leading you to believe you are the smartest person in the room.

Seed: Open communication will support innovation and critical thinking.

Seed: Strive to surround yourself with employees with skills and wisdom outside your expertise.

I have been in more meetings than I can count, I am sure some of you can relate to this. And I have been in meetings that my opinion mattered, at least I was led to believe my opinion was important. Some managers go into meetings with decisions already made and attempt to give an appearance of involving the team in the decision making process. This eventually becomes apparent to the team and results in a loss of respect.

Seed: Be genuine, be authentic, and honesty goes further than manipulation.

Seed: When attempting to get the buy-in of the department, have evidence prepared to support the change is necessary for the success of the organization.

A department that is managed by someone that does not trust or respect the team will eventually push employees out of the department. The image of the department becomes faded, it will not attract the best talent, and it could take years of damage control to rebuild the reputation of the department and the trust of the employees. If the department's manager is the destructive force in the department, the organization needs to take action to remedy the situation. The rebuilding of a department depends on upper managements support.

Seed: Do not become the destructive force in your department because of your insecurities. Your team will support you if you trust and respect them.

Seed: The culture of the department is directed by the leaders of the organization, lead by example.

Seed: The value of your team deserves recognition, pay it forward when you look good, and invest in a tune-up when the team is not running on all cylinders.

Chapter 3

Attitude vs. Behavior

I thought I landed my dream job, I was paid well, had an amazing retirement and benefit package, and I felt my skill sets were being utilized which made me believe I was valued.

My first salary increase was half as much as I was promised during the recruitment stage of the hiring process, I was under the impression my manager lied to me. After two years of working for the organization, animosity developed between my manager and myself, promises were broken; trust and respect diminished, and I resented going to work.

Seed: Do not make promises you cannot keep, do not use the carrot on the stick method to entice employees.
Seed: When salaries cannot be raised, paid time off and work schedule should be flexible.
Seed: Mistakes are made by managers and employees, showing you can forgive will allow employees to accept your faults as a manager and strengthen your relationship.

Feeling as though this was not my dream job anymore and I knew I could do better. As the result of the communication between my manager and myself, I did not feel appreciated, he did not support my efforts for a promotion, and our working relationship was not one of trust and respect. My previous employer contacted me and made me an offer to come back to work for them at the right moment; I quit my dream job and went back to my previous employer. The decision I made was based on my resentment for my manager and not one based on what was best for my family and myself.

Seed: Leaders need to reinforce a positive productive perception of the department, reassuring employees recognize their importance and realize the rewards beyond the monetary value.

Seed: Employees perceptions become their reality, leaders need to support a positive and productive perception.

Seed: When evaluating employees performance, leaders need to focus on the results of employees and not the feelings of the manager.

Almost every organization has one individual that is never happy, always complaining, who likes to gossip, they create ciaos any moment, and sometimes it is the manager that is the toxic integer. The reasons for this attitude, they may fell undervalued, overwhelmed, disliked, not included in decision-making, or their ego and pride has given them a sense of being irreplaceable and they felt like the company would fail without them. We cannot read the minds of others, but we can identify what someone believes about the company by the comments they make and their actions.

Seed: Negative thoughts are developed within our own insecurities and need to be tuned out.

Seed: Choose to say positive comments about others even when others are focused on the flaws.

I started a new position at an organization that was the largest company that I have ever worked for. One of my coworkers seemed to take an interest in me and was quick to tell me the gossip in the shop. One thing I have learned is to keep quiet when someone is gossiping, gossip does not support a productive department. As time progressed, I recognize the dynamics in the department; it was not productive or trusting. A few sour apples had tarnished the reputation of the department. What had guided the direction of the culture in the department was pride, ineffective

communication of the production process, incivility, personal insecurities, entitlement, lack of training, and lack of engagement. Emotions of employees can be detrimental to the success of the department, if the employees are disgruntled, dysfunctional, and cannot work with each other. Time and money will be wasted on EEO complaints, investigations, mitigation, and possibly the hiring process. *Seed: Team building events need to be planned and tailored for the department.*
Seed: When the negativity is apparent, bring out the issue into the light and extinguish it.
Seed: Finding the root cause of the destructive culture and addressing it needs to be a priority.

The perception of certain employees was that the only way they could get ahead was to find reasons to justify overtime. Because certain employees are motivated only by money, once they have reached the top step of their position, they may lose the drive they had to be productive. *Seed: Before employees top out in their positions, they need to identify their purpose as a necessity within the department.*
Seed: Leaders of departments need to shape the perception of the employees to envision success as a team effort of individual contributions leading to organizational success.
Seed: People are complex but they also have a lot in common, they want to be respected and valued.

When leaders are able to show how the efforts of everyone determine the results of the department, employees recognize their importance and realize their value. Getting employees to identify with ownership of the process they are responsible for will allow employees to understand how the effort of every employee can elevate or diminish productivity. When an employees realize how important they are to the process of production and how they support the organization, they are motivated to support the department beyond the salary compensation. *Seed: When employees have ownership over their process or product, they are motivated beyond the salary compensation.*

19

Seeds of Leadership

Take a moment and focus on what motivates individuals that serve in church ministries and mission trips, volunteering in the Peace Corp, and are open to helping those in need without any financial reimbursement. They do it because they believe in serving others and recognize a higher purpose than serving themselves!

Seed: Leaders need to connect the efforts of employees assigned duties to a higher purpose of serving others.
Seed: Associating ownership with on-the-job accomplishments reinforces trust and respect.
Seed: Caring for the success of others is a passion that drives leaders, the lack of caring is a lack of commitment.

Working with a diversity of employees requires the capacity to be flexible and patient. Relationships within the workplace need to be managed, in order to have a relationship based on trust and respect, time and effort are required as an investment from management to employees. When management takes the time and effort to cultivate trust and respect within the department, management's ability to lead becomes easier.

Seed: Emotional investing redeems rewards of support within the department.
Seed: Being flexible is necessary when navigating relationships within the department.
Seed: Creating a budget for team building exercises and creating activities once a month will payoff in more ways than one.

While working for a cabinet shop in the 80's, I had the opportunity to work for someone that had a dysfunctional relationship with his wife and step kids. He had quit his position working for the county of Riverside and started his own business. I am not sure if it was the stress of the business or other reasons why their relationship was failing and they were getting a divorce. My manager took me to breakfast on a Saturday morning before opening the store as an appreciation breakfast. I never forgot that he kept the store closed to have breakfast with me. This act of kindness demonstrated appreciation and I felt valued. I wondered if he showed acts of kindness to his wife and made her feel appreciated.

Seed: Everyone has an emotional bank account, we make withdrawals and we need to remember to make deposits!
Seed: Demonstrated appreciation goes along way and is not easily forgotten.
Seed: In marriage two become one, when the department works together as one it is highly productive.
Seed: Our working relationships become another form of family.

When management does not take the time and effort to develop working relationships with their employees, employees will have the mindset of management not caring about the individuals and believe that management only cares about results and productivity. In turn, this leads to a mindset of employees only caring about the paycheck.
Developing the mindset within the department towards one of supporting each other and caring about their efforts of the department supporting the organization in a direction of accomplishing the vision of the organization is possible with taking the necessary steps of encouragement. Encouraging everyone to support each other strengthens the abilities of individuals when achieving the goals of the department.
Seed: People need to be encouraged as the rudder guides the movement of a ship to the destination.

When I was younger I believed that a challenging career would be the one to master, and would have the least amount of competition in workplace and thereby having higher pay and job security. Electronics seemed to be highly technical so I enrolled in an electrical trade school immediately after I graduated high school, at the same time I was employed as a tool and die apprentice. Tool and die seemed to be more challenging than electronics and I applied myself to the Tool and Die trade of machining. What I discovered as time past, people and relationships can be the greatest challenge if you lack the social skills to navigate situations and attitudes.

Seed: Social skills are a necessary component of leadership. People are more challenging and complicated than electronics, machines, and any other trade that exists. People are unique; their uniqueness makes them more valuable than any machine. We have emotions and perceptions; our perceptions generate our beliefs, which become our reality.

If we believe we are working under misdirection, falsies, and a lack of leadership, this becomes our reality.

Seed: Changing the perception of others is the greatest challenge, especially if you cannot change who you are for the best of others and the organization.

Seed: Encouragement is necessary to reinforce the bond of trust between a manager and employee!

Chapter 4

Momentum Towards Change

When I was in my twenties, I had taken a college course called Marriage and Family Relations. I thought it was going to be a good place to meet girls, a lot of other guys thought the same way. This course covered the subject matter of raising children, domestic challenges, and communicating with your spouse. When raising children, on occasion they require positive and negative reinforcement, followed by love and expectations. Very similar to employees, but the expectations of employees are communicated clearly and attainable before the error is made, at least they should be.

Seed: Leaders that show empathy with their expectations will have better results than setting expectations without.

Seeds of Leadership

Seed: When managers focus on the faults of employees and fail to recognize their accomplishments, employees become discouraged and disengaged.

Management that uses their authority to assert respect will lose the ability to lead others. Leaders that communicate expectations clearly and effectively. Management that manages with intimidation, authority, and focuses only on negative reinforcement will not have the ability to lead the team. I have seen a department go from being static and disengaged to becoming dynamic and engaged by the change of management.
Seed: Creating momentum toward a positive and productive working environment begins with change.
Seed: If you expect better results, you better evaluate your delivery.

A fruit tree needs to be pruned to bear fresh fruit, just as a department needs pruning when bad fruit is falling from the tree. Sometimes it is the manager that needs to be plucked from the department so stronger roots can form. If you cannot pull the weeds out, you can choke them out by planting new employees with the right work ethic and mindset.
Management needs to recognize the importance of employees, as more than being assets, employees need to understand that they are key components of the larger mechanism. Momentum begins with changing the mindset from attaining individual success to achieving organizations goals and serving customers.
Seed: When we are willing to sacrifice our personal wants for the needs of others; we are presented with more opportunities and resources of becoming a leader.

Baby steps to changing a department's mindset results in employees crying like babies. Momentum is dynamic inertia, it is a body in motion, and once it is moving it becomes easier to keep it moving, (Newton's Law). If a department is changed too slowly, the friction of certain employees in the department could prevent the momentum from gaining traction.

23

Seed: Leaders need to validate the reasons for change to the team.
Seed: When employees understand the purpose of the direction that the boat is headed they will either be on board or be left at shore.

Changes should be directed on what is best for the department and the organization. There is not a reason to mislead employees that decisions are made to make their job easier; this will result as an attributing reason of losing trust and respect. Earning the respect of the team demands illuminating the truth, do not shade the truth!
Seed: Employees are smart, be truthful and respectful!
Employees recognize appreciation; appreciation could be in the form of buying lunch, creating an afternoon of an activity that works on team building, spending time getting to know your team shows you care about them. Recognition could be used as a tool of appreciation, appointing someone to employee of the month with some kind of reward creates competition to perform.
Seed: Employees are encouraged by leaders when given a challenge and trusted to complete that challenge.

Chapter 5

Perception of Employees

I have a friend named Tony, in the 80's he worked for a large dealership in Riverside California; he was the executive manager overseeing all the departments within the dealership. He led others to become the best at what they did for the company. The mindset he instilled upon the sales department was, "the customers had to believe that they were getting the best deal that exists." When sales performance was high it was reflected in the pockets of the employees, he had improved the lively hood of the department. When Tony relocated to another dealership, employees followed him. The employees followed him because of what he did for them.

Seed: Employees follow leaders because of what the leader did for them.

Our reality is generated from our perception, just as the customers believing they were getting the best deal. We naturally want the best deal for a purchase and want to be paid a premium for our employment. If we perceive we are in a dead-end job, that we are not significant, this becomes our reality.

Everything in life has what is known as a standard or a baseline, this is a point of reference to compare current conditions. In the maintenance field we use the (baseline reference) when performing predictive maintenance. Measuring the wear of tire tread and comparing it to the thickness of the tread when it was new is an indication of proper alignment, tire pressure, and driving characteristics. By these measurements you can predict the life of the tire and do a cost analyze in reference to time and usage. Comparing our income, position, and potential of growth to other positions in the company establishes a baseline of reference. We are either above or below the line. This comparison can impact our perception of happiness and thereby affects our health, demeanor, productivity, and loyalty to our current position. Managers can use this to predict the employees' performance and engagement.

Seed: The grass/culture is greener on the other side of the fence because they water and use fertilizer/encourage and equip.

Seed: The Benjamin's cannot be the only bait attracting and keeping the talented employees.

Seed: When employees realize that the lure from one company to another is more than money, the manager could be the deciding factor to keep talented employees!

Seeking out ways to cultivate the culture within the department is as fertilizer is to grass it produces positive results. When management focuses on developing a positive perception of a department, employees will believe in the department's success. Employees believing in the success of their department believe they have achieved personal success.

Theory #1, department's success is defined by the achieving performance standards required by customers.

Theory #2, department's success is defined by the perception of upper management.

Reality, organizational success depends on the ability of every department being able to support each other in achieving departmental success, which leads to organizational success.

The combined results of different departments achieving organizational success should be the goal. When we are able to rely on the support of others within the organization we have a stronger ability to be productive, if we believe others in our department are going to support us, we have the perception of a collective force that is able to accomplish any challenge.

Seed: Many hands make light work, and the wisdom of counsel is wiser than the mind of one.

Chapter 6

Self-Awareness

It was Monday morning and the manager of the department shows up late. The manager would talk about the difficulties of home life and consistently came to work sick and/or failure to eat breakfast made her highly irritable. Monday meetings were highly unproductive, the objectives of the week hidden in between blankets of misdirection and irrelevant information. The emotional instability was reflected in the managers inability to separate emotions and actions during the decision making process within our department. Meetings would go from 0-60 from calm to screaming.

Seed: When we demonstrate self-control, others control themselves.

Seed: Leaders need to abstain from reflecting the emotions of others and allowing their emotions to influence the decision making process.

Leaders need to recognize their triggers of stress and emotions. Identifying the triggers, understanding methods, and the mindset required when responding to these triggers. Understanding your emotions and how they could affect others and affect your ability to lead the department. Lacking the ability to control your emotions will lead to the inability to lead your team effectively and effect your ability to make sound decisions.

Seed: Professional fighters control their emotions during a fight, an emotional fighter is a fighter destined to lose the fight.

Self-awareness is being able to recognize our strengths and weaknesses. Recognition of what we need socially, emotionally, and spiritually in order to being successful at developing relationships is an asset of personal growth and reward. We may naturally be technically strong but socially weak. Social intelligence is having the ability to communicate in a way that invites conversation, interest, trust, respect, and the ability to build strong relationships. Building dependable relationships is a necessity of leadership, when going into battle you will fight side by side with someone you honor.

Seed: Leaders have inherited charisma and genuinely have a love for developing relationships.

This love is an attribute of sincerely caring for others, supporting others, and empowering others with the abilities and resources to succeed, these are attributes of leaders.

Seed: Putting your employees needs above your wants for the benefit of others and/or the organization is a quality of leadership.

While working for an organization that lacked leadership, I recognized a number of factors that impacted my ability to be an effective instructor. The factors were a lack of references and resources. When I presented these challenges to my supervisor, my supervisor said it was my job to work with them and work around them.

Because of my manager's lack of expertise of the subjects taught, she did not support/trust the instructors when making purchases for better training equipment.

Leaders need to possess a level of confidence, confidence in their staff's decision-making process and confidence in the team. Departments led by individuals that lack confidence of their capabilities to make sound decisions will lead to delays, obstacles of momentum, and decrease productivity.

Seed: The lack of confidence of making sound decisions could be from lack of experience, rely on the expertise of those you selected to surround you and support the department.

Chapter 7

Responsibilities

Observing the departments manager showing up hours late and going home an hour early every day, impacted the commitment within the department. When you are the leader you should walk the walk of the leader. Leadership is dedication to the department by showing up early and being the last to leave. Setting an example of what you expect from your employees creates the model for employees to follow. Your actions and how you present yourself shows your commitment and dedication to being the leader of the organization.
Seed: Do not have expectations of others that you would not expect of yourself.
Seed: As the leader you should care about the health of your staff.

Stress is a factor of management, it is your responsibility to maintain your health, be proactive and not reactive when it comes to your health. Realizing you cannot control others, you can guide them by providing the vision and direction required to attain the goal. As the leader of the department you will have expectations of employees and when they fall short of your expectations, you will need to evaluate your delivery of expectations, are you clear and specific?
Seed: Your health is more important than worrying about the imperfections and failures of others, stay in your lane, find success in a failure!
Seed: As the leader of the department you should know your team; taking the time to show a genuine interest in the goals

*of the employees and the personal/professional
achievements in life.*

Leaders need to develop open communication within the department. Open communication is driven by trust; it is projecting an open door of transparency in communication, this will encourage trust among the team. If your team trusts you they will feel open to discuss ideas and/or concerns. Ideas and/or concerns could develop into generating more profit, processes becoming more efficient, and safety concerns being address that could reduce workman's compensation claims.

Seed: Trust is essential to receiving respect; respect is required to be an effective leader.

Seed: Someone may respect your title and position but not respect the person in position.

Seed: A department with an open door policy will communicate more effectively.

When mistakes occur, leaders need to recognize the lesson to be learned from the mistake for future precautions. Lessons learned from mistakes should not be the only education leaders receive; leaders need to take classes constantly to improve their ability to lead others. Leadership is a lifelong passion of evaluating ones self and continually seeking ways to improve upon ones abilities.

Seed: The lessons of life never stop, humility is recognition of being imperfect and willing to listen and learn. Recognize the opportunity to learn from a mistake!

Chapter 8

Engagement

Some managers are required to develop employees as part of their assigned goals and expectations, and leaders develop members of the team because they care and desire to encourage others for future opportunities.

When Henry Ford created the assembly line, production increased, it was cost effective, and maintained the level of quality the company desired. Employees on an assembly line became experts at limited tasks. By limiting the amount of critical thinking and/or assigned goals, the employees at Ford, knew how to accomplish their assigned tasks. Employees that are not required to use critical thinking and problem solving skills could be paid less. But, this also led to employees becoming unsatisfied and disengaged because they did not believe they were important and they would seek out other opportunities.

Creating engagement within the department begins with developing others. Team members' supporting each other creates a department of engagement. When employees are willing to share their knowledge and experience with others on your team, it creates a culture within the department that is supportive and successful.

Seed: Employees that eagerly seek out opportunities to help fellow employees develop their skillsets and knowledge are employees that demonstrate leadership qualities.

When leaders of the department support development it creates a culture of those within the department desire to develop others. Developing your coworker's abilities will not develop you out of a job, it will show your leadership qualities of elevating others to help them in their current position and future positions.

Seed: Leaders that fail to develop others, fail to support their team. The developing of employees could have a domino effect on the team's performance.

Management that is reluctant of supporting others is most likely not equipped to be in leadership positions. Encouraging others is a win-win situation, when others are equipped to be better in their current position; it develops a higher competency within the department, results in an increase in production and quality.

Teams within the department are components of a larger mechanism known as the organization that create a product or provide a service. When building a motor, if you were to improve one component of an engine and left the other components stock, the overall performance would most likely not change. But, if you upgraded all the components and they were designed to work together, the increase in performance would definitely be apparent. *Seed: The culture of a company is like the performance of an engine, all the components work together for top performance or it needs to be overhauled!*

Developing individuals to become more compatible with others creates collaboration; collaboration is a collective effort, which is much stronger and wiser than the efforts of any leader alone. We all have inherited abilities, experience, and education that bring value to the team. When a leader can harness all the employees' strengths to work together, the team is able to produce results that benefit the department and the organization. *Seed: When you recognize the weakest link in the chain, give them opportunities to become stronger.*
Seed: Leaders realize the potential of the employees and seek out opportunities that will challenge the employee and create an engaged employee culture.

Chapter 9

Commitment

While working for a gun manufacture, it became apparent that management did not tolerate any nonsense from their employees. Employees were easily dismissed and quit because of the lack of leadership within the organization. Management made it clear that a skeleton crew could come in and do the job as well as the current employees. This statement discouraged commitment and loyalty did not exist. It became apparent that the employees were not valued.

Leaders need to recognize employees as assets to the organization, (not as an asset depreciates but as one that is an investment).The longer an employee is employed in the same position for the same employer, their experience and knowledge enables them to be more productive, less mistakes, and better results. Commitment and loyalty is necessary in order to keep employees from leaving for other opportunities. Having employees quit for other opportunities creates obstacles with the current production process and possibly huge issues of lost information leaving with the employee. Especially when the one leaving is leaving with extensive experience acquired while working for the organization that is needed for cross-training new employees.

Supervisors that develop good working relationships with their employees foster commitment, employees feel obligated to perform at a higher level than employees that dislike their supervisor. If the person in charge is disliked, not respected, and is not trustworthy, employees will have less commitment of arriving to work on time, keeping the manager informed of issues with the production process, and employees will be less likely to give ample notice when a new opportunity exists. Employees want to follow leaders that treat them as assets. *Seed: Actions speak louder than words, showing you value, respect, and trust your employees will foster commitment.*

Chapter 10

Assets

When we have valuable assets, we must monitor, protect, maintain, and assess the value of the assets. People require monitoring in the form of communication and personal investment, (getting to know your team members personally). Protect them from the politics of upper management, protect them from developing toxic attitudes, and protect them from becoming complacent.

Seed: Developing ways to measure the pulse of the employees engagement will allow you to recognize the when you need to make a deposit, an emotional deposit.

Emotional deposits are necessary in relationships. As leaders we need to make deposits so when we make withdraws it does not affect the perception/attitude of the staff. Maintenance of employee's attitudes requires team-building events such as weekly luncheons, monthly events, and yearly celebrations; little recognition will go a long way when it is sincere. And it is the leaders responsibility to assess the competencies of everyone in the department. If the team is not becoming more productive, increasing of quality, and making fewer mistakes, the team may need additional training. The level of training from within the organization has a cap; it would benefit the department to hire a training resource from the outside.

Seed: Assets generate revenue, liabilities generate cost.

Employees that are not productive and providing services to meet the organizations goals are liabilities. Employees are paid a salary to serve the company for a determined amount of time, employees provide a service and by providing this service they accomplish tasks to meet the organizations goals. The revenue generated by the organization far exceeds the salaries of the employees, which makes the employees assets to the company.

Seed: Educating, equipping, and challenging employees will support your employees to transition from a liability into an asset.

Chapter 11

Relationships

Once in my career I had a manager say to me, "we do not have to like each other to work with each other." As my supervisor made this statement I realized, this person really dislikes me. The reasons of her animosity is not important, what is important is that my supervisor let me know she did not like me. I was hurt and discouraged because the statement led to me believing my supervisor did not value my experience and expertise to support the department. Hostility, harassing, and passive aggressive behavior became the normal tempo of communication from my manager. This led eventually to me leaving the department.

Seed: You may not recognize someone's presence, but you will recognize their absence. Positive recognition is necessary feedback that employees need!

Seed: We will have employees that have faults, which go against the grain, and have personalities very different from our own.

Seed: Do not allow how you feel about someone effect the way you support him or her as an employee!

Managers that have the propensity to assert their authority and bully their employees will eventually lose employees that are top performers. Insecure managers are driven by emotions, emotions that will eventually drive out valuable employees.

Managers that push out the top performers tend to replace them with employees with similar mindsets that are not top performers and thereby drive down the department's ability of performance.

Seed: Good working relationships are required within a department, just as oil is required to reduce the friction of moving components in a mechanism.

Friction between coworkers and between management impacts the ability of the production process by hindering momentum. Developing good working relationships within the team is the responsibility of the leader of the department. Leaders need to develop team-building exercises and create ways to generate trust and respect between employees.

Seed: Exercise is necessary to stay healthy, team-building exercises is necessary to maintain a healthy working relationship!

Joking is an acceptable dynamic if everyone has the same sense of humor and if the joking is not disrespectful or demeaning. The leader of the department has to make a point to emphasize that incivility will not be tolerated, that humility will be valued, and those who support others in the department will be rewarded. During the hiring process, hiring managers need to identify personalities that will work well with other employees.

Seed: Leaders need to be authentic, respectful, and trustworthy when developing relationships with your employees.

Every meeting and conversation with individuals in your department is a series of moments that will strengthen or diminish working relationships. If a majority of meetings with an employee were discussions of the lack of achieving departmental goals, the employee would associate the manager's presence with negative feelings and will develop resentment. As a result, communication with the manager would become ineffective because of the perception of the employee feeling defensive. This perception is generated by the pattern of progressive negative conversations that occurred between the employee and the manager.

Seed: Good working relationships enhance the ability of effective communication.

Seed: Sandwich the good with the bad and finish meetings with the positive which will leave the employee feeling positive. And when making the sandwich do not use the word (but) when you say "your doing a great job but", it spoils the positive note.

38

Seed: When faced with problems focus on the solution, once the solution is achieved determine the root cause of the problem.
Seed: Be open to being wrong!

Chapter 12

Results

It was 1988, I had a 71 Camaro and I wanted to rebuild the motor, it was a Chevy 350. My stepdad was a diesel mechanic and worked on large heavy equipment, we had all the tools required to do the job. I had read Hot Rod magazine since I was 10 years old, so I had a basic understanding of the components and how they worked. I was sixteen, I did not have a large budget working part-time in a machine shop and going to school.

We disassembled the motor and assessed the parts, recognizing we had a good foundation to work with, (the engine block). After cleaning everything and purchasing parts I knew the selection of parts had to work with each other. Meaning, the lift of the cam, size of valves, type of manifold, size of carburetor, and exhaust manifold had to work together and control the flow of air and fuel following through the motor. The right selection of components would develop high performance and dependability; the wrong selection could be a waste of money and cause issues with performance.

This was done with gas was still .99 cents a gallon. My Camaro was getting about 15mpg and I was spending about $20 every three days on gas. I was able to get close to 15 seconds in a quarter mile and I thought it still was not fast enough. The problem was the gearing, plenty of power but not able to put it to the tires fast enough.

Seed: Discover, Plan, Act, and Review.

When the hiring manager is going through the selection process they need to be mindful of how the selection of talent will work within the department. Having superstars for employees is great as long as the superstars are willing and able to develop others that are not as experienced and/or educated. Creating a team with individuals that are cohesive cultivates a culture of performance. Each employee has specific responsibilities and when all the employees are able to accomplish their responsibilities to their manager's expectations and help others exceed their expectations; it increases the overall performance of the department. Departments that communicate effectively, generate the best results.

Seed: When employees are able to complement each other, the performance of the department becomes elevated. High performance engines perform better than stock because of the combined effort of all the components working together!

Results of the departments need to be directed at accomplishing the goals of the organization. When managers are able to combine the organizations goals with developing positive working relationships of employees, the culture of the organization will become engaged.

The department's accomplishments are a reflection of the manager's ability to manage. Poor results within the department are attributed to a lack of leadership. When employees lack clear direction they can lose focus on attaining the departments goals.

Seed: Achieving more production/results, can be achieved when the manager has supported the development of positive working relationship within the department.

Chapter 13

Remembered

Have you ever met someone that had more interest in you than you had in them? When around a group of strangers do you engage others in conversations? When you meet someone do you listen to understand and desire to know him or her? These are traits of someone that enjoys the company of others. To successfully lead a team, you will need to become personal with every person on the team; this will be more difficult for an introvert than an extrovert.

I recall working for a gentleman that never engaged in small talk, never spoke about anything personal, and distanced himself from others on the crew. He was very experienced and had a strong technical background, but he never laughed, smiled, and was often sick. He was working in a position that did not coincide with his natural behavior. After a few years he was demoted to his old position and replaced by another person.

A few months later I had a talk with him and he said he was much happier to be back in his old position. *Seed: When we are in positions of authority and lack social skills, relax and listen to understand before responding, give recognition of accomplishments in public, and counsel in private.*

The new manager was an extrovert; he was a people person and was socially intelligent. Showing up to work in a button up shirt, pocket protector, and a ruler was not the average dress code I have seen with other managers. He would say good morning everyday before I could say good morning to him, and everyday started with a smile. Dave was his name and he turned out to be the first leader I have had the opportunity to work for. Dave ate lunch everyday with the crew and would talk about his life outside of work and developed personal connections with everyone on the crew. When Dave was hired, employees from his previous employer contacted the company and enquired about employment. I will always remember Dave as the leader I inspire to become; he was fair, sincere, genuine, honest, and pleasant person to be around.

Seed: The managers that stood out as leaders leave the impression of genuinely enjoying people.

Seed: When you have the responsibility to lead others, how do you want to be remembered?

Chapter 14

The Finish Line

In the 80's I was working in a engine shop building type 1 Volkswagen motors, I built an 1835cc, dual Dellorto carbureted beast of a motor for my 1965 Karmann Ghia. While at the parts store (Save A Bug) in Riverside California, I saw an ex-coworker from the engine shop. This one was difficult to work with, he did not support other employees, and acted like a Mr. Know it all. He challenged me to a race, we both had the same size motor and he raced at the track on the weekends. I did not think I would win but I had to try to shut this guy up. I had taken the seats out of my car and lowered the tire pressure in the back, we raced and I won. His engine had more power than mine and his tires were spinning, my car put the power to the road and I was faster. Everyone from Save-A-Bug saw the race and that guy could not talk any more smack.

Seed: Working together you will have greater results than competing against each other.

Seed: Recognizing the strengths of others and developing positive working relationships is preparing for success when the opportunity exists.

Chapter 15

Extra Seeds

A few seeds that I wanted to include that need to be sprinkle into the soil of culture:

Seed: Leaders accept responsibility when the department fails to reach department goals, and gives credit to the crew when the department achieves the goals!

Seed: Employees can't accomplish a given task because of lack of training or experience, or they won't because of attitude.

Seed: Every conversation can build or teardown trust and respect.

Seed: Have a heart of compassion for those that surround you they look up to you.

Seed: When speaking in front of an audience, envision whom you are reflecting.

Seed: Enthusiasm is contagious!

Seed: Be informed by your situation, not transformed.

Seed: Take time to reset your emotional clock between interactions.

Seed: Evaluations are tools used to inspire employees; conversations with constructive criticism before and after an evaluation are used to encourage employees.

Seed: To think anyone is replaceable is a mindset that everyone is equal in value, if this were true, training and experience would have no value.

Seed: Coaching is a trait of leadership; employees need to understand the benefits of being coached!

Seed: Employees are muscles and to build a stronger department, everyone needs to be stretched and rested.

Seed: When empowered with leadership, lead with an open hand and not a closed fist.

Seed: Kindness and forgiveness are essential for culture cultivating.

Seed: Lessons of life can be difficult, but they make the pleasant memories stick even stronger.

Seed: The worse and the best managers stand out for what they did to you or for you.

Conclusion

These are seeds that took over thirty years to collect, seeds that will bring collaboration, commitment, engagement, and enthusiasm into the workforce if planted correctly and watered with support.

The first step to culture reform is caring about those that surround you at work. Do not wait until change becomes a necessity because of the loss of talent and experience.

I apologize for the editing errors throughout this publication. I did not write this to be recognized as a writer. I wrote this short read to help new managers, old managers, and the one's that do not know that leadership is rated by the heart of the one in authority to trust, equip, and inspire those that surround him or her.